I0819322

better together*

* This book is best read together, grownup and kid.

a
kids
book
about

a kids book about GENDER AFFIRMING CARE

by Lindz Amer

A Kids Book About
Editor Emma Wolf
Head of Design Rick DeLucco
Publisher Jelani Memory

DK
Senior Production Editor Jennifer Murray
Senior Production Controller Louise Minihane
Managing Editor Hazel Eriksson
Publishing Director Mark Searle

This American Edition, 2026
Published in the United States by DK Publishing,
a Division of Penguin Random House LLC
1745 Broadway, 20th Floor, New York, NY 10019

26 27 28 29 10 9 8 7 6 5 4 3 2 1
001—357811—May/26

First published in Great Britain in 2026 by
Dorling Kindersley Limited, 20 Vauxhall Bridge Road, London SW1V 2SA
A Penguin Random House Company

The authorised representative in the EEA is
Dorling Kindersley Verlag GmbH. Arnulfstr. 124, 80636 Munich, Germany

A CIP catalogue record for this book is available from the British Library

ISBN 978-0-2418-0081-2

Printed and bound in China

www.dk.com

akidsco.com

This book was made with Forest Stewardship Council™ certified paper – one small step in DK's commitment to a sustainable future.
Learn more at www.dk.com/uk/information/sustainability

This one's for Frank! You're the best decision I've ever made—except for my wife, Hilary, who is very cool too.

Intro
for grownups

You probably felt a certain way when you saw the title of this book. Maybe you felt shocked, grateful, uncertain, or curious. No matter what, I'm glad you opened it. I hope I can destigmatize this topic for you and the kids in your life, and provide a helpful resource for those who need it.

You see, "gender affirming care" is a term most people have heard, but few actually know what it means! That's why I'm here. Because gender affirming care can encompass so many things, and it probably isn't exactly what you think it is.

Gender affirming care can be taking on a new nickname or getting a haircut. It can be about finding community and building support systems. It can involve doctors, medicine, and surgical procedures, but that's just a tiny piece of the whole pie.

The fact is that *everyone* can (and will) take a bite out of the gender affirming care pie, sometimes without even knowing it! Let me show you what I mean...

Hi! I'm Lindz! I wrote this book!

I have three sisters.

I love to sing and play soccer.

I use they/them pronouns.

MAYBE you have siblings, too?

MAYBE you like to play
music or sports, too?

MAYBE you've met someone who
uses they/them pronouns, too?

Maybe

YOU

do!

I didn’t always know all of these things about myself.

I had to discover them.

When I was a kid,
I loved wearing **THIS** pair
of green corduroy overalls.

I've got the biggest SMILE on my face, right?!

But then there are other pictures, like **THIS ONE** with my sister.

I know that smile is FAKE.

I remember there were a lot
of times when I felt pressure
to be a certain way.

But every time I wore something
or did something for someone else…

I was always

UNHAPPY.

The first time I cut my hair really short is when I felt like myself.

Maybe for the **FIRST** time ever.

I met other people who had short hair just like mine, and who liked to kiss girls, just like me.

Some of them

NEW and INT

words for the

used

ERESTING

mselves.

Like

"nonbinary"

or

"gender nonconforming",

and pronouns like

they/them.

I asked my friends to start using they/them pronouns for me, too.

And I discovered that...

I told my friend Teddy about being nonbinary on our YouTube channel,

QUEER KID STUFF.

When I told Teddy, I told
a lot of other people too.

It was **EXCITING** and **SCARY**,
all at the same time.

I remember looking at a picture of someone with these cool scars on their flat chest. And I felt jealous.

I wanted a flat chest just like theirs.

I got **TOP SURGERY*** three months after my thirtieth birthday, and it's the best present I've ever gotten.

*If you're curious what this is, chat about it with a grownup!

It took me a long time
to get here. But I’m finally me.

My BEST, most TRUE, most AUTHENTIC version of me.

I'm probably not done discovering everything about myself.

BUT I'M SO

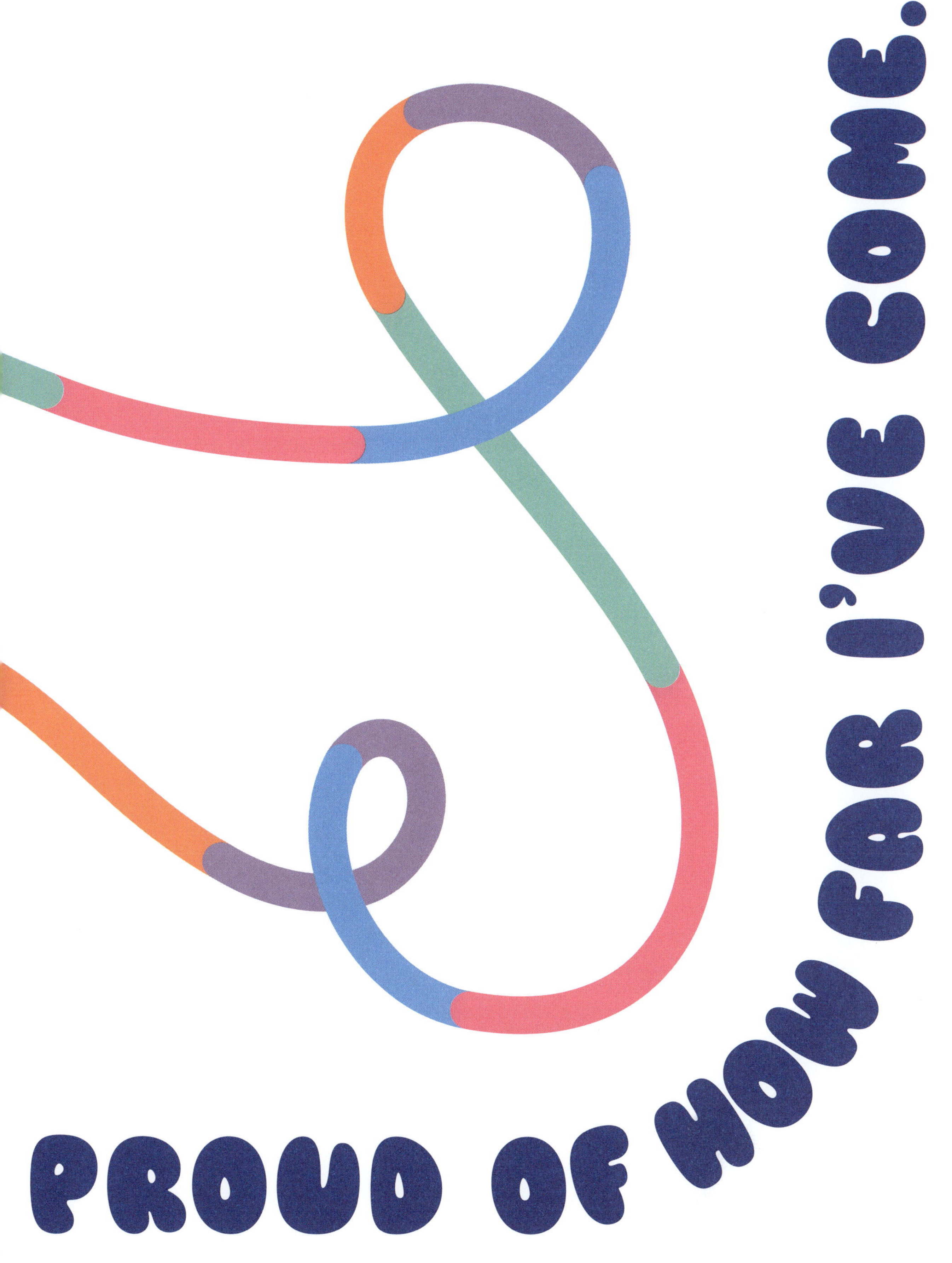
PROUD OF HOW FAR I'VE COME.

My journey of self-discovery doesn't exist without something called **GENDER AFFIRMING CARE**.

GENDER AFFIRMING CARE is a process.

It's all about figuring out how you feel on the **INSIDE**, and how that can show up on the **OUTSIDE**.

Gender affirming care

YEAH, EV

is for everyone!

Sometimes, gender affirming care is about how you

EXPRESS YOURSELF.

Did you know
that getting your hair cut is gender affirming care, whether it's short, long, pink, or blue?

Did you know
that you can pick out clothes from any section of the store, no matter how they're labeled?

Did you know
that painting your nails or getting your ears pierced* is something you can do to express yourself?

*With a grownup's support!

EVERYONE,

no matter who they are, has the right to feel good in their body.

Sometimes,
gender affirming care is

INVISIBLE.

Did you know
you can use lots of different
words to describe yourself?

There are pronouns like
she/her, **he/him**, **they/them**,
e/eir, **per/pers**.

Or words like
nonbinary, **transgender**,
or **gender nonconforming**.

There are endless options!

Did you know that you can find other people who like the same things as you?

People who like to **SING**, or **PLAY SOCCER**, or **COOK**, or **DANCE**, or whatever *your* favorite thing is!

And **DID YOU KNOW** there are professional therapists you can talk to about how you are feeling, whether you are happy, sad, or feel like you don't quite fit?

I’ve been in therapy for a long time, and it’s helped me a lot!

EVERYONE,

no matter who they are, has the right to figure out what makes them happy.

Sometimes,
gender affirming care is

MEDICAL.

Did you know
that doctors can help someone who is losing their hair as they grow older, regrow it?

Did you know
that doctors can help kids pause puberty, so they can decide how they want their body to develop as they grow up?

Did you know
that grownups can get surgery to change or reshape their bodies, so their outsides reflect how they feel inside?

Like my top surgery, which reshaped my chest!

EVERYONE,

no matter who they are, has the right to feel at home in their skin.

Gender affirming care is normal and has been around for a really long time.

Some people don't think that's true.

Some people believe that...

you have to have your
hair a certain way,

or you can only play certain sports,

or you must live in a certain body,
even if it makes you unhappy.

Imagine what the world would be like if everyone had access to gender affirming care.

I think everyone would be a lot **HAPPIER**, don't you?

That's why

GEN

AFFIR

CA

DER
MING
RE

is for...

EVER

YONE.

Outro
for grownups

I told you my story—now it's your turn! Who are *you*? How have you already accessed different types of gender affirming care? Are there other kinds of gender affirming care you'd like to try out?

Self-discovery is all about trying new things and seeing how they fit. Maybe you'll like it, maybe you won't. That's all a part of the journey! And lifelong journeys are better together. Thanks for bringing me along on yours.

About The Author

Lindz Amer (they/them) wrote this book because a lot of people don't understand what gender affirming care actually is and why it's awesome! It can even be life-saving!

In 2015, they created a YouTube series called Queer Kid Stuff with their best stuffed-friend, Teddy, where they explain LGBTQ+ topics for kids. They wrote a book for grownups called *Rainbow Parenting*. They also wrote a picture book called *Hooray for She, He, Ze, and They* about pronouns and how words make you feel. They've also done some other pretty cool things, like creating the first nonbinary character in the *Paw Patrol* universe.

They write songs and stories and perform for families all over the United States. See you at their next storytime!

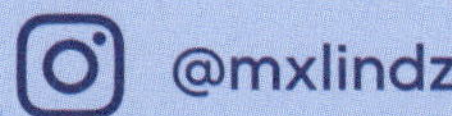

 @mxlindz  www.mxlindz.com